curious about
JUNETEENTH
BY DR. ARTIKA TYNER
AMICUS LEARNING

What are you

curious about?

CHAPTER THREE

Let's Celebrate!
PAGE
16

Curious About is published by Amicus Learning, an imprint of Amicus
P.O. Box 227, Mankato, MN 56002
www.amicuspublishing.us

Editor: Ana Brauer
Series Designer: Kathleen Petelinsek
Book Designer and Photo Researcher: Sara Hood

Library of Congress Cataloging-in-Publication Data
Names: Tyner, Artika R. author
Title: Curious about Juneteenth / Dr. Artika Tyner.
Description: Mankato : Amicus Learning, 2026. | Series: Curious
about holidays | Includes bibliographical references and index.
| Audience: Ages 6–9 | Audience: Grades 2–3 | Summary:
"Discover the importance of Juneteenth! Learn about Juneteenth's
history, significance, and celebrations in this question-and-answer
book for elementary-aged readers. Includes table of contents,
glossary, further resources, and index"— Provided by publisher.
Identifiers: LCCN 2025014074 (print) | LCCN 2025014075
(ebook) | ISBN 9798892008471 library binding | ISBN
9798892009133 paperback | ISBN 9798892009799 ebook
Subjects: LCSH: Juneteenth—Juvenile literature | African
Americans-Social life and customs—Juvenile literature | Enslaved
persons—Emancipation—Texas—Juvenile literature | Enslaved
persons—Emancipation—United States—Juvenile literature
Classification: LCC E185.93.T4 T96 2026 (print) | LCC E185.93.
T4 (ebook) | DDC 394.263—dc23/eng/20250523
LC record available at https://lccn.loc.gov/2025014074
LC ebook record available at https://lccn.loc.gov/2025014075

Photo Credits: Alamy Stock Photo/ZUMA Press, 11, 15;
DVIDS/2nd Lt. Ebony Bryant/U.S. Air Force, 5; Getty Images/
Amanda McCoy/Fort Worth Star-Telegram, 10, Chip Somodevilla,
16–17, Drew Angerer, 12–13, FRANCOIS PICARD, 2, 8–9,
Gary Coronado, 3, 21; Library of Congress/ Carpenter, F.
B. (Francis Bicknell), 6; Shutterstock/Lightspring, cover, 1,
Tippman98x, 19, Visuals6x, 2, 14; The Noun Project/Roaming
Grove, 22, 23, Zach Bogart, 22, 23; Vecteezy/Omprakash
R, 20; Wikimedia Commons/Mathew Benjamin Brady, 7

What is Juneteenth?

Juneteenth is a holiday that celebrates the end of **slavery** in the United States. It honors Black people who were brave and never gave up. They fought to be free. It reminds us to keep fighting for freedom and justice for all.

DID YOU KNOW?
The name Juneteenth comes from the date of June 19.

Juneteenth is celebrated
on June 19 every year.

What happened on June 19?

On January 1, 1863, President Abraham Lincoln freed many enslaved people with the Emancipation Proclamation.

Enslaved people in Texas were the last to learn that they had been freed after the Civil War. It took two and a half years for the news to reach them. **Union** General Gordon Granger brought the news on June 19, 1865.

In 1865, Gordon Granger brought the news of freedom to Galveston, Texas.

Why did it take so long to share the news?

A mural in Galveston, Texas, tells the story of Juneteenth.

Texas was a slave-holding state. Texas wanted to keep Black people as slaves. It did not share the news that slaves had been freed. Texas also ignored the Thirteenth Amendment, passed in January 1865. It officially ended slavery in the US.

Who is the grandmother of Juneteenth?

Opal Lee's "Walk for Freedom" happens every year.

Opal Lee. At 90 years old, she started walking to support Juneteenth becoming a national holiday. She went to more than 20 states. In each state, she walked 2.5 miles (4 kilometers) for each year it took the news to reach Galveston, Texas.

Opal Lee worked hard to make Juneteenth a national holiday.

When did Juneteenth become a national holiday?

In 2021. People from across the US fought for justice. They wanted change. The Juneteenth National Independence Day Act was passed by Congress. It was signed into law by President Biden.

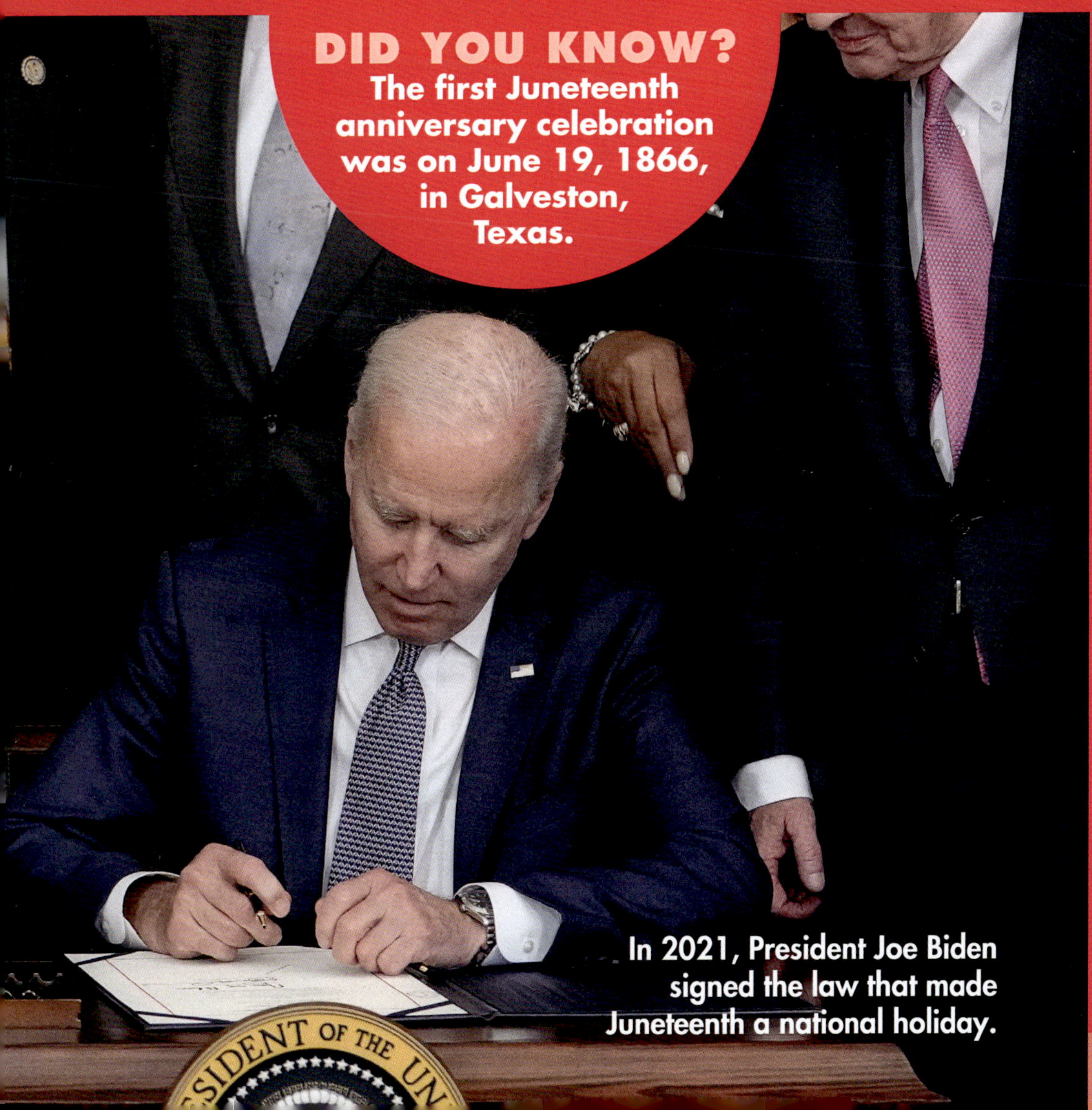

In 2021, President Joe Biden signed the law that made Juneteenth a national holiday.

What colors are used for Juneteenth?

Green, black, and red. These are the colors of the Pan African flag. The flag stands for freedom from **colonialism** and **racism**. Green is for the land. Black is for the community. Red is for the people who fought to be free.

The Juneteenth flag stands for freedom and a new beginning.

DID YOU KNOW?
Juneteenth also has its own flag. It is red, white, and blue. The star stands for Texas.

CHAPTER THREE

3

How do people celebrate Juneteenth?

HARD WORKERS

People eat red treats on June 19. Red stands for the sacrifice of the Black community on freedom's journey.

People celebrate with parades and events. They come together and eat **soul food**. Others gather for concerts, a rodeo, or a Miss Juneteenth contest. Some people create plays to share about Black history.

Many cities across the country hold Miss Juneteenth contests.

Who celebrates Juneteenth?

The Black community. They celebrate to honor their **ancestors'** strength. But anyone is welcome to celebrate Juneteenth. It reminds people that the fight for racial justice continues. It reminds people to acknowledge the past and promote equality for Black people.

Kids learn about history and freedom on Juneteenth.

Is Juneteenth celebrated around the world?

Yes! African Americans bring the tradition with them when they live in other countries. They celebrate their history and culture. They hold parades and musicals. They also gather for community dinners and barbecues.

WHERE IS JUNETEENTH CELEBRATED?

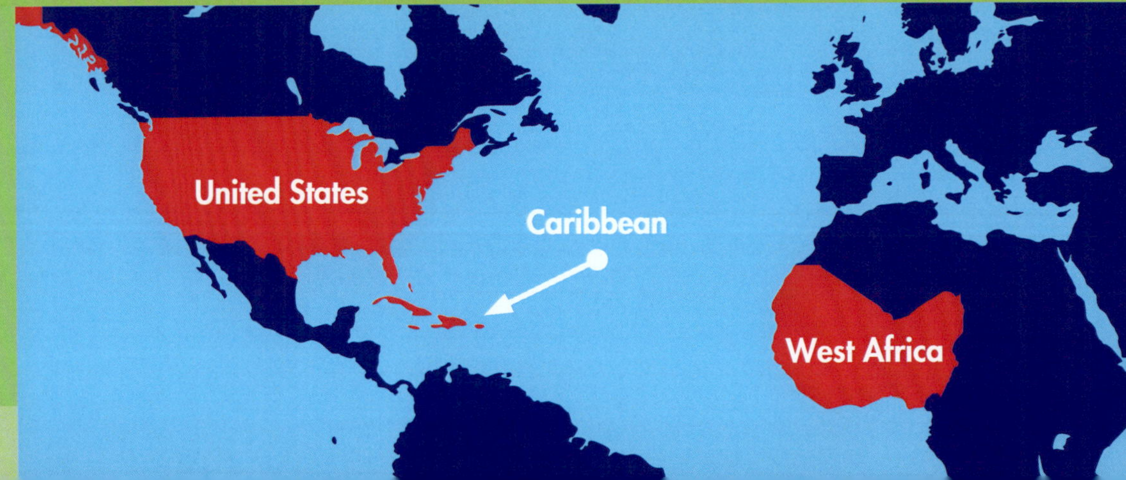

Dancing and music are part of Juneteenth celebrations in many cities.

ASK MORE QUESTIONS

What is freedom and justice?

How can I host a Juneteenth celebration?

Try a BIG QUESTION: Why is Juneteenth known as the Second Independence Day?

SEARCH FOR ANSWERS

Search the library catalog or the Internet.
A librarian, teacher, or parent can help you.

Using Keywords
Find the looking glass.

Keywords are the most important words in your question.

?

If you want to know about:

- what freedom and justice mean, type: FREEDOM AND JUSTICE

- hosting a Juneteenth celebration, type: JUNETEENTH PARTY

FIND GOOD SOURCES

Here are some good, safe sources you can use in your research.
Your librarian can help you find more.

Books

J is for Juneteenth
by Jamariah Cross, Kimani Prince, and Ariyah Webster, 2024.

Juneteenth: A First Look
by Katie Peters, 2023.

Internet Sites

Britannica Kids: Juneteenth
https://kids.britannica.com/kids/article/Juneteenth/632532
This site provides information about Juneteenth and its history.

National Geographic: Celebrating Juneteenth
https://kids.nationalgeographic.com/history/article/celebrating-juneteenth
National Geographic Kids is an educational website for kids. Learn more about Juneteenth.

Every effort has been made to ensure that these websites are appropriate for children. However, because of the nature of the Internet, it is impossible to guarantee that these sites will remain active indefinitely or that their contents will not be altered.

SHARE AND TAKE ACTION

Support a local Black-owned business.
Ask a friend to go with you.

Go to a Juneteenth event in your community.
Participate in the learning activities.

Choose a favorite song about justice and freedom.
Share it with others.

GLOSSARY

ancestor A person who was in someone's family in past times.

colonialism When one country takes over another country.

racism Treating people unfairly or badly because of the color of their skin or where they come from.

slavery Owning people against their will.

soul food The cultural food of the Black community.

Union Non-slaveholding states during the Civil War.

INDEX

About the Author

Dr. Artika Tyner is a passionate educator, award-winning author, civil rights attorney, sought-after speaker, and advocate for justice. She lives in Saint Paul, Minnesota, and is the founder of the Planting People Growing Justice Leadership Institute.